D1507877

The meditations and writings of:

"Fill your paper with the breathings of your heart."
—William Wordsworth

FEATURING THE DESIGNS OF BEN KWOK

You just got exciting news!
Who's the first person you tell? Why?

What was your most successful New Year's resolution?

You run into your time-travelling future self.
What do you ask yourself?

What have you worked the hardest for?

How do you cheer yourself up?

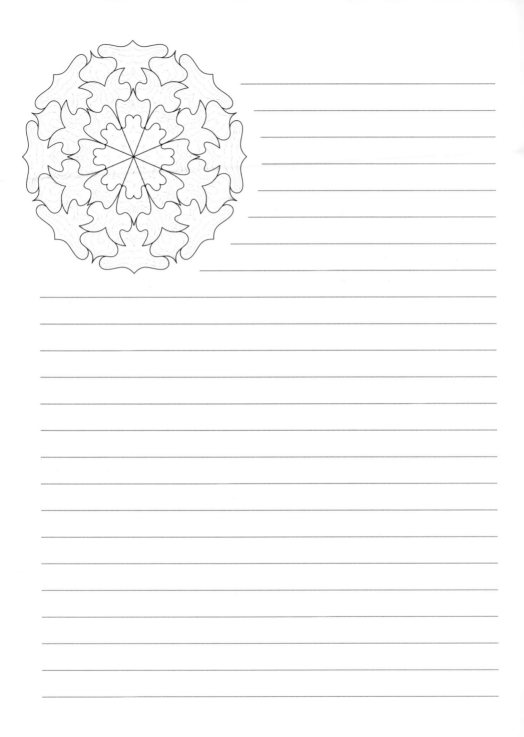

Love or money?

What have you stopped yourself from buying recently?

You have an unexpectedly free day.
What do you do?

What was the best meal you've ever had?

Whom are you grateful for?
When was the last time you talked to them?

What are three things you can see right now that you like?

_____

_____

_____

_____

_____

_____

_____

_____

_____

_____

_____

_____

_____

_____

_____

_____

_____

_____

_____

_____

_____

_____

_____

What is your go-to activity when you want to procrastinate?

Dogs or cats?

What was the last compliment you gave someone?
How was it received?

What color is your mood today?

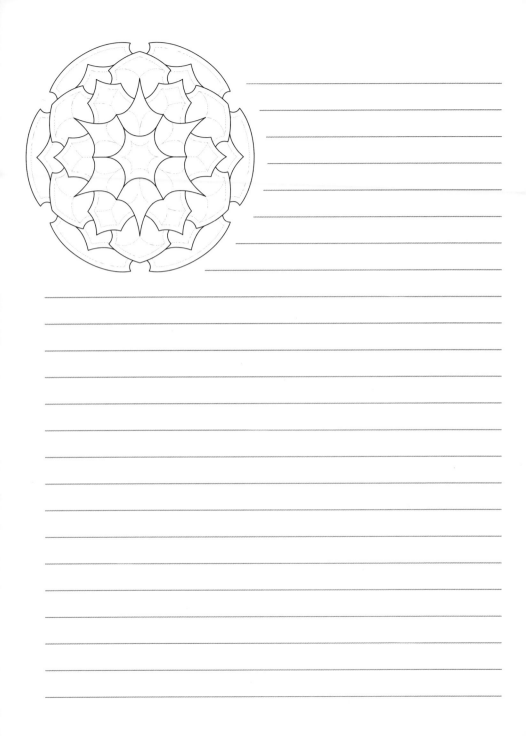

When was the last time you cried? Why?

What did you want to be when you grew up?
Did you change your mind along the way?

_____

_____

_____

_____

_____

_____

_____

_____

_____

_____

_____

_____

_____

_____

_____

_____

_____

_____

_____

_____

How would your best friend describe you?
Your mother? Your pet?

You find a magic lamp, and the genie inside offers to change one thing in your life. What do you choose?

What kind of friend are you?

What is the best scent on Earth?

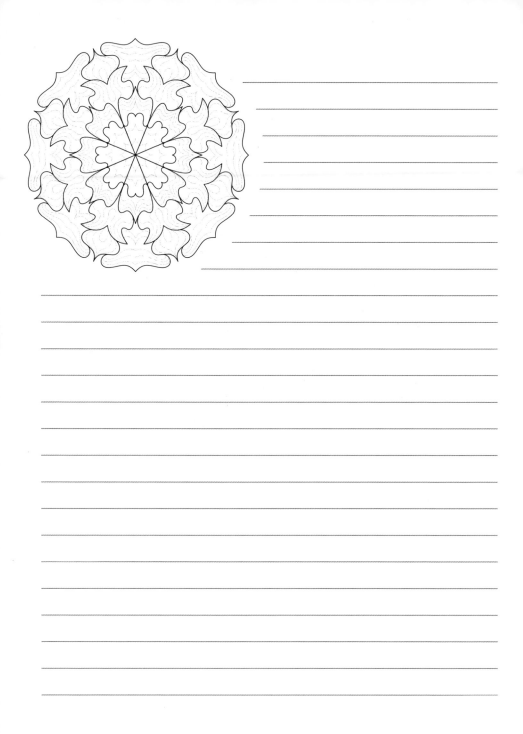

What is a class you would like to take?

What are you the best at?

You just got a promotion! How do you celebrate?

What animal is most similar to you?

You can send your teenage self a letter
with one piece of advice in it. What is it?

What's the best thing to do when you're at home during a thunderstorm?

Set a goal for next month. Set a goal for tomorrow.

_____

_____

_____

_____

_____

_____

_____

_____

_____

_____

_____

_____

_____

_____

_____

_____

_____

_____

_____

_____

_____

_____

_____

What makes you unique?

What is your earliest memory?

If you could have dinner with any three people, alive or dead, who would you choose?

Who is your biggest hero?